BOA
EDITIONS LTD

T0160940

USEFUL JUNK

USEFUL JUNK

poems by

ERIKA MEITNER

○ ○ ○

AMERICAN POETS CONTINUUM SERIES, NO. 191

BOA EDITIONS, LTD. ○ ROCHESTER, NY ○ 2022

First Edition
22 23 24 25 7 6 5 4 3 2 1

For information about permission to reuse any material from this book, please contact The
Permissions Company at www.permissionscompany.com or e-mail permdude@gmail.com.

Publications by BOA Editions, Ltd.—a not-for-profit corporation under section
501 (c) (3) of the United States Internal Revenue Code—are made possible with
funds from a variety of sources, including public funds from the Literature
Program of the National Endowment for the Arts; the New York State Council on
the Arts, a state agency; and the County of Monroe, NY. Private funding sources
include the Max and Marian Farash Charitable Foundation; the Mary S. Mulligan
Charitable Trust; the Rochester Area Community Foundation; the Ames-Amzalak
Memorial Trust in memory of Henry Ames, Semon Amzalak, and Dan Amzalak;
the LGBT Fund of Greater Rochester; and contributions from many individuals nationwide.
See Colophon on page 104 for special individual acknowledgments.

Cover Design: Sandy Knight
Front Cover Art: "Masculine Still Life" (powder coated steel, stoneware, brass), 2021, by
    Genesis Belanger, photographed by Pauline Shapiro.
Back Cover Art: "Hostess" (stoneware, porcelain, fabric), 2019, by Genesis Belanger, photo-
    graphed by Pauline Shapiro.
Interior Design and Composition: Richard Foerster
Manufacturing: McNaughton & Gunn
BOA Logo: Mirko

Library of Congress Cataloging-in-Publication Data

Names: Meitner, Erika, 1975- author.
Title: Useful junk / poems by Erika Meitner.
Description: First edition. | Rochester, NY : BOA Editions, Ltd., 2022. | Series: American poets
    continuum series ; no. 191 | Summary: "A master of documentary poetry, Erika Meitner takes up the
    question of desire and intimacy in her latest poetry collection" — Provided by publisher.
Identifiers: LCCN 2021044285 (print) | LCCN 2021044286 (ebook) | ISBN 9781950774531
    (paperback) | ISBN 9781950774548 (ebook)
Subjects: LCGFT: Poetry.
Classification: LCC PS3613.E436 U84 2022 (print) | LCC PS3613.E436 (ebook) | DDC 811/.6—dc23
LC record available at https://lccn.loc.gov/2021044285
LC ebook record available at https://lccn.loc.gov/2021044286

BOA Editions, Ltd.
250 North Goodman Street, Suite 306
Rochester, NY 14607
www.boaeditions.org
A. Poulin, Jr., Founder (1938–1996)

Contents

"Whoever you are, now I place my hand upon you, that you be my poem . . ."

—Walt Whitman

O

"What defines desiring-machines is precisely their capacity for an unlimited number of connections, in every sense and in all directions."

—Gilles Deleuze & Félix Guattari

O

". . . the light contained in every thing, in every surface, in every face."

—James Baldwin, on painter Beauford Delaney

I would like to be the *you* in someone's poem

I would like to be the *you* in someone's poem so I can say I'm not even kidding they're playing "Those Were the Days" by Mary Hopkin on the Kroger sound system and that song reminds me of my dead grandmother and the way she'd sing the *dy dy dy* bits in her Yiddish accent at joyful family events and here I am getting a little misty at the register

I would like to be the *you* in someone's poem so I could also explain that when I got back into my car with groceries the radio was playing "Footloose" by Kenny Loggins and I immediately thought of Lori Singer and her dangerous red cowboy boots and the way dancing can lead to fucking according to every small-town preacher on film

But really I would like to be the *you* in your poem—especially if there's a car on fire we can rubberneck on a bus trip through an unspecified city or maybe a rooftop bar with cocktails that always have one mysterious ingredient requiring inquiry like Elisir Novasalus or Punt e Mes

Especially if I'm in a parking lot at night at one supermarket or another again sitting in the driver's seat of my car typing itinerant messages to you in your poem

The messages say *Wonder* and *O say can you see*

They say put me in your fictional poem because we are all fictions, because the way the hot driveway feels on my bare feet when I go get the mail at 5 p.m. is not real—not the walking or the heat stored up all day then emitted from cement or the paper in my hands addressed to me

Because the way I open the box twice to make sure I haven't missed something exciting is also not real

Once there was a spider's nest in there plump with eggs and another time the rain got in and smudged the name of the renter still taped to the bottom and x'd out in ballpoint

X me out of your poem once you put me in—draw a line through my name or disguise it as part of our country: *O America you never fail to disappoint me*

Your choice in leaders your ignorance your racism your crescent moon tonight low and bright over the Appalachians

There are many wrong things in this world and nothing is not complicated, but just once I want a poem to have second-person me in it and come from somewhere else—be generated by a machine I have nothing to do with

There's a breeze out on the stoop tonight at dusk but I don't really know this as I'm otherwise occupied in your poem doing something I don't yet know about

Like watching the neighbor kid setting off pink fireworks at the end of his driveway, the shower of sparks and purple stars at the end cracking the dark wide open, then vanishing

Letter in the Time of Junkmail

Dear _____,

I've got the sky in my mouth so when I open it to speak
nothing leaks out except contrails. I order my coffee

and it comes to me in a robin's-egg blue cup with my name
scrawled on it in black marker, almost spelled correctly.

Sometimes when I think of you—I can't help it—I shake
like a carnival ride or an earthquake of minor proportions.

I've got years in my mouth too, waiting to be fished out,
laid across a table, and gutted. Sometimes at restaurants,

to entertain my kids, I twist paper straw wrappers into tight
snakes then make them dance by dropping water on them

bit by bit. It's a slow drip, like an under-sink leak, and they
twirl up like pale strippers on a pole, like flowers unfurling

in time-lapse video, the way I'd like my heart to open, rote,
without hesitation. Look, I have trouble saying anything

aloud. Slit me open like a seed pod or an envelope.
Unfold me like a credit card offer, a recall pamphlet,

an explanation of benefits, this endless paper desire coming
and coming from somewhere, sprawling like all of suburbia

across a landscape, but I am not fleeing the bumping-
against energy and hard concrete. I am unafraid of

the way the heat rises from city sidewalks in July and August,
curbs sweet with piss and trash and unwashed skin ripening

with whatever makes us feral. I want to rub up against slick
subway tile, feel my back pressed to a bathroom stall door

in a bar where the band is playing no one's favorite song
about yearning, or nostalgia, or sadness with a hand

down my pants, all the unspeakable parts of us
rubbing until the contrails dissolve in the sky,

our paths untraceable, letters still arriving in bulk
and unbidden with my name mostly spelled right

in the see-through windows, with the amounts I still owe
out-of-pocket outlined in neat black type mass-produced

by some machine who knows the things only I do
about my eyes, my skin, my blood, my heart.

Selfie with Airplane Voyeurism & References to Your Body

The woman across the aisle from me
reading *The Celestine Prophecy* has a
tattoo on her foot in Latin but I can't
make out the exact phrase as I am not

magic or wearing my glasses. Before
boarding, I ate a sausage biscuit in a
plastic clamshell at a table where
we were all plugged in to a greater

current, charging our appendages.
I close my eyes and when I open
them again we are still on a runway
waiting for the propellers to lift us

past the tarmac. *Alis grave nil.*
The clouds as we rise sit low over
the warehouses and electric towers
holding up wires to the sky as offerings.

We travel across them as pixels,
uncladded rooms of light carved
from rock, naked mess of cable
and tendons, construction of bone.

Luceat lux vestra. Your skin. I drove
all morning through a fog so thick
the highway was a twisted white
sheet. I tailgated an 18-wheeler,

red signals outlining its container
as it sped. Steel-clad body. Body
cutting the fog. It's actually 4/20
and everyone should be high and

holding a bowl of something in our
lungs or hands. Everyone should be
looking out the window hoping for
more spring, which is glorious if

you are loved or love yourself.
The woman reading *The Celestine
Prophecy* is filming the girl next to
her in the window seat who is

freaking out on the ascent with joy
and fear and awe combined, saying
wow wow wow wow. This plane
is not rote for her. I've seen

your body over and over on screen,
carpe noctem, and I am headed
toward you, your inimitable tattoo
flush with trouble. The most famous

quote from *The Celestine Prophecy*
is this: *We must assume every event
has significance and contains a message
that pertains to our questions*. What

should I ask? Here I am throttling
forward, temporarily indenting a space
of plastic and foam, where the body
has a total lack of concealment

or shame. How can a body resist
the forces pressing against it?
Later, what will the girl think
of that recording, her mouth

an O of wonder and terror
and pleasure?

The Seeming Impenetrability of the Space Between

(after Colin Blakely)

Your message says *I still remember what
your pussy tastes like*, and I blush then
delete it stat, because there's no way,

after twenty years, that you can conjure
that sea of whatever, the down-there-
in-the-dark—not with all the bodies

we've put between us. Whatever's
passed into you, through you, from
then until now: you can keep it.

My secret is still your starched shirt-
tails entwined with your half-erect cock,
the tile on my back, what the woman

who saw us coming from the ladies'
room all those years ago when she was
going in must have thought. My secret

is that no matter what you might tell me—
the two girlfriends in Miami, the OxyContin
addiction (now kicked), that your wife

thinks you're in Philly—all of it—I don't
give a shit. When we were young and
stupid, and maybe beautiful as a beer bottle

shattered on a moonlit sidewalk, we'd
fuck all night and I knew if I opened you
below the rib-cage you'd be filled with

jewels or whatever gave off the most
light, so if we made out like bandits
stealing time back, if you paused

to press your forehead to mine in guileless
moments—if our breath caught in
the gears of our chests, your hands

on my breasts and everything shooting
off sparks, it seems possible to skip
forwards and back in time at once

because none of the fundamental laws
of physics that govern the Universe
state that time has to go in one direction,

—that even if we're arrows pointed at
the sky, or a target, or a road winding no-
where I can follow you, we're drawn to

entropy, disorder, a release of energy,
from the Greek *entropia*—a turning
toward—our bodies in that bathroom

stall—when an incoming train, still
invisible, lights up the end of a tunnel.

All the Past and Futures

(after Valerie Roybal)

is an incorrect construction because it implies
that we only have one past and many futures

and if I know anything it's that our pasts are
multitudinous and wild and overgrown with

weeds, and our futures might converge in
some field with an abandoned hotel where

we'll sit on the edge of the cracked / empty
pool with its peeling blue paint and recount

all the ways we forgot to touch each other
gently because we spent so long asleep

and turned away from whatever time held
in her sweating hand (a lug nut, a twist tie,

a rubber band) offered to us flat and with-
out affect to bind our wounds together, you

ether, me either, whisper just a descriptor
of where you plan to put your fingers (in my

mouth?) (in my palace of wonders?) I want
to say *cunt* but the hard consonants don't fit

and here I am saying it anyway and you're
yelling *don't do that don't ruin a thing of time*

and beauty and don't you worry about how
scattered memory gets (pick-up-sticks, a box

of buttons, shards of plastic beached across
an entire coastline) and how we're just trying

to find the origin, the place where, on an axis
y meets x?

Seven Fragments About Christmas and an Episode
of Night Swimming

(after Ed Ruscha)

Drive Thru Live Nativity says the sign next to the Arby's on North Franklin.

Walmart, I kissed the sounds of the register, the registers kissed me.

Your jumpsuit of distress. Your mask of sadness.

There's a billboard with a real camel and a girl dressed like an angel, and it says, This adventure will take you back in time.

We went night swimming at a Holiday Inn one time in Louisville in our underwear.

Your one-stop shop!

A shimmer of possibility.

It says, You will experience first-hand the birth of our Savior, featuring live animals and professionally crafted scenery.

Something about being architects of our own beauty.

Every child brings its own luck, said my grandfather, and our mouths are always apocalyptic.

It was at the wedding of the friends who introduced us, though now they're divorced. We drank cheap beer and swam all night in the hotel pool and security never came for us.

Only a risen savior can save a dying world.

Endure. Swifter than we expected.

Please tell me, my love, that something else is possible.

The world is beautiful: nine swimming pools and a broken glass. Some duplex apartments. Thirty-four parking lots. Twenty-six gasoline stations. Every building on the strip mall.

Before morning, we returned to our rooms.

Médium Adam 25

On the hotel's terrace in the rain I smoked
an illicit cigarette, tried to record a poem
but the recycling truck's clink and glitter;

but the wind cycling through the palms.
Before that: the dive bar with bathroom
graffiti—*condoms don't protect the heart*

on the ladies' room toilet paper dispenser
and *they sure don't* on the wall beneath it,
then the whole bar singing John Denver's

"Take Me Home, Country Roads." I came
from the mountains, hips thrust forward,
for warmth and commerce. I came for my

body's momentary impression in the sand.
No good can come from this neon center-
fold bar filled with strangers and lovers.

No good can come from the bodega after,
with its fluorescence, its couples stumbling
in, entwined, to peer at rows of beer and

yogurt behind glass. I am not an abstracted
self in the wet night. I am not a static
enterprise either, and as I move through

time and space, many things are vanishing
in exchange for a wanting with no end that
takes up residence inside me like a squatter.

Since I have no home here, I drive through
neighborhoods photographing For Rent signs
staked in lawns before entering a museum

with a Carolee Schneemann photo of herself
as Eve—look at the way snakes straddle
her breasts, how her lush 70s bush

runs up her belly. The skin of your room
must be breathless—I can taste the salt
and spit. This trip, I am all the daybreak hotel

beds in South Beach, Ocala, St. Augustine,
covers peeled back, pillows slightly dented.
Lover / Stranger you are not here and I miss

you—your body in every building, frame and
scaffolding, in the shushing of cars driving
the causeway, in the cigarette butts loosed

from lips and stubbed out in the sand, in the
hole of every doorway. If I execute works
in the dark by mouth would that be considered

an intervention? If I put my finger in whatever
divot? Yet no illumination is available. Yet
to lie down and become invisible, even under

the camera's eye. Yves Klein's blue women
pressed their nude bodies against sheets
of paper at his command. And his blue is not

night sky, not rubbed out dusk over the bay
stocked with cruise ships—definitely not the
moon under sodium vapor glare, even if it is

a Super Blue Blood Moon tonight hanging
above every neon parking garage in Miami.
Those women's bodies left behind a rocket ship,

a flower with wilted petals and erect pistil
(or is it stamen?), a blue-on-blue dildo with
a skirt around it. Yves, listen: we are making

art because we want to inhabit everything
and not fear it. Yves, we are television sets,
and how can I touch you—you're so far away.

We are all singing *take me home*, my head
on your bare chest, my hand down my own
pants. The bar, the screen saver, the night

where the air is like skin, a black hole, an
aperture, open, opening—my body a barrier
against light.

Eternity Now

When the cathedrals were made of plastic,
my hands, I didn't know what to do with them.

They roved & roved my body like benevolent
mosquitoes or drones or skiffs trawling the bay

at sunset. Air is 830 times lighter than water—
even when the Earth was formless and empty,

even when the Earth was absence and salt.
To execute an intention means to abolish

a desire, means this scripture is a form of
reckoning—a recovery of my body & your body

as concrete, as forms of unchecked development.
Look, I refuse to break with the numinous universe

when I cross the eruv: string drawn across the tip
of South Pointe Park bounding the community

whose edges murmur *what have we survived* &
how are we held to account? Open up

for me, you say but what you mean is be the
undulating skin wrapped around scaffolding

inhaling / exhaling, catching anything loosed
by construction. The most beautiful thing is to be

un-present; to be extended, not in breadth,
but more & more upwards. Everything depends

on the tower crane, on where you stand &
the long shadow of a building—not a dwelling,

not a cave. Winch me up. I can taste your
certificate of occupancy, your semen & spit—

my hands moved upon, my mouth swept.
You are inextricably altering the façade

of whatever you touch, says the city to us, like
god who created 310 worlds before this one

with fluttering & hesitation over the face
of the deep since what does it mean not

to inhabit but to cross the threshold of this
void, this jewel box, this whole Earth just once.

Elegy with Lo-Fi Selfie

I am thinking of you while riding shotgun past the Celanese plant
at dusk mid-December this sprawling factory on the New River

the world's largest producer of cellulose acetate tow used in
cigarette filters lit by sodium vapor the plant glows orange-

tipped the smokestacks smoking like us on the stoops & curbs
of Brooklyn years ago is the most cliché way to turn back time

in a poem those Marlboro filters ringed with my lipstick yellowed
with our inhales we'd pass one back & forth some nights I hold

my phone to my face & its light makes me glow blue as a specter
or a television in the neighbor's window I think of you too when

on my way home I pull in to the Kroger to look again at my phone
in the dark this lit thing in my hand pulsing you are not on the other

end you've been dead for years died before phones could take photos
check emails connect us to networks of what I am not the only one

sitting quietly in my car as the moon shifts behind the ABC the Great
Clips eclipses half the lot when me & another woman are swallowed

by the automatic doors then try to separate two half-size carts because
neither of us wants a giant wagon to shudder us down the aisles but

we can't pull them apart then I realize I've left the house in leggings
as pants since she's in them too & there's my ass visible I think it's

still tight I have no point of reference I'm over forty but the cashier
cards me anyway for wine says *you could be my mom* says *you look*

so young I look so young there's a millennial in the cereal aisle who's
maybe eyeing me & another guy shopping in leg gaiters & crampons

even though we only got four inches of soft powder this morning which
melted quick since this is the South the supermarkets are out of milk

I want to tell you about the crampon guy you'd laugh so hard because
in college remember New Hampshire winters some days our scarves

welded to our lips froze to our cheeks with just an inhale's vapor
your breath your breath is gone & now I want to take a picture

of my ass to send to you because I think you'd think it was hilarious
or sexy or possibly both but I can't reach my ass & you're dead &

if I tried to take a sexy selfie I'd probably just look like a body they
find in a dumpster on an episode of *Law & Order: SVU* I'm still sitting

in my car looking at my camera flipped around to mirror my own face
made lo-fi static by a filter the New River is one of the five oldest rivers

in the world but no one who doesn't live here knows this I live here
& I am stuck in my car thinking of you somewhere, Chris, I am taking

this snapshot & posting it on Instagram I am inhaling slightly
parting my lips moistening them then touching my finger

to the button & it clicks & clicks

from this thought a hazy question

(after Margaret Ann Withers)

my friend who lives in the mountains and I talked on the phone yesterday
when she was on break from finishing some plumbing in a guest house
she's refurbishing because her job quit her and there's the divorce and
she needs the rental cash and we were talking about illness and poetry
and her formidable skills with sexting and secret loves and she says
men see women's bodies not the way we see our own bodies, with the
scars and misshapen bits and hanging flesh, but as gifts, as wrapped
things filled with pleasure and surprise and I knew as soon as she said it
that she was right based on the way my imaginary lover might write *hot*
and *fuck* and *my god, that ass* if I sent a decent picture of my ass which could
take me months to figure out because taking a selfie of your own ass requires
some dexterity which is in short supply with me and I don't know really
how to take a compliment either so I'd just send more photos which is
ill-advised because this is the internet and we all know what can happen
to photos on the internet since we weren't born yesterday but in the 70s,
actually, and my friend postulates that none of us Gen X women know
how to take a compliment because we came up in a *Reality Bites* cynical
era of Doc Martens 'zine feminism and independence though I think it's
not just us because in the women's bathroom of the college where I teach
taped to the doors of the stalls are signs in turquoise and pink cursive marker
from Omega Phi Alpha sorority that says *Hey you! Take a compliment!*
and when I tell my friend about my self-conscious c-section scar, she
tells me how her secret lover is hung like an amateur porn star with this
hugely unexpected cock and what do you do with something like that
other than fuck it and now we're onto HPV and condoms and she says
you have to have the awkward talk neither of us have had in years—
the one that says *I try to protect my body*, and I tell her about the other

night when I had my first cigarette since 2007 and it was better than
I remember anything being—an incandescent American Spirit I bummed
from my friend Wayne on a bar porch and there I was smoking in the
warm March evening while traffic shushed past on Main Street, the tip
lit like a taillight then vanished to ash like a car driving off in the dark
each time I inhaled and can I ask you again to tell me about my body,
to introduce me to my own luminous skin?

Nude Selfie Ode

Listen, you didn't ask me to do this but what I want to tell you is that I wish we had this kind of technology years ago, because instead of calling one night to say meet me on the corner of Henry and Court where we sat on the curb and I said I actually like you that way and you said you didn't I might have just sent a photo

You would have sent one back (or not)

I still worry about where they might end up

"The concept of 'the beautiful'," says Wittgenstein, "has caused a lot of mischief." (Marjorie Perloff)

Another ex who is not dead and in Dubai writes me after Iftar and too many gin and tonics to say when he moved to the suburbs he would walk around the lake near his house and yell into the wind as loudly as he could

In retrospect this was a sign that maybe his marriage wasn't working

His message says *I almost sent you a photo, but it was inappropriate*

In the morning he writes *I'm sorry—I was drunk*

"Desiring-machines are neither imaginary projections in the form of phantasies, nor real projections in the form of tools." (Gilles Deleuze & Félix Guattari)

In the morning when the house is empty, I aim for posterity

I don't know who you think you are, the photo says

The photo says *I'm beautiful and have some regrettable tattoos*

The photo is taken in the best possible light

The photo is taken from above

The photo is taken with my back to the window so I have a halo

Outside the clouds are low and diffuse in the trees

The photo is taken with the self-timer

I don't care if the neighbors who shoot and four-wheel at the same time see me

The photo has a serious filter

Lark, Reyes, Juno, Slumber, Crema, Ludwig, Aden, Perpetua, Amaro, Mayfair, Hudson, Valencia

A composer I'm collaborating with found out that I secretly love the band Asia, so he held his phone to the mic in our 3D black box sound space and let "Heat of the Moment" play from all 138 speakers

Those power chords at the start of the song are the same as loving your own broken-down body—the holy jolt of electricity, then the way the song settles into itself, mellows but still preens a little at the bridge

"An act of touch may reproduce itself as an acoustical event or even an abstract idea, the way whenever Augustine touches something smooth, he begins to think of music and of God." (Elaine Scarry)

A look from you and I would fall from grace

Objects become larger when you move the phone closer—for example, my ass becomes Kardashian in lace and my cleavage an endless National Park canyon, until I remember none of this is real—just pixels

Architect Ludwig Mies van der Rohe popularized the phrase *less is more*

In the best one, my face is turned away and my hair falls over my breasts

In the best one, I am touching myself

Secret ecstasy—I am shameless

"I look at you and a sense of wonder takes me." (Homer, *The Odyssey*)

In the best one, my mouth is open when I come

I keep it for a month in the trash on my phone and sometimes I pull it up and look at it after I park my car in the Target lot

Everyone around me is always looking at their phones too

Their faces are turned toward the light

Victor Turner called it *liminality*

This is the threshold of the world

We go through this doorway and we are changed immeasurably, illuminati, things of wonder and desire

my body my body my body

"An object, already within the horizon, has its beauty, like late luggage, suddenly placed in your hands." (Elaine Scarry)

Aubade with Projector

(after Tala Madani's "Shafts" & "Sex Ed by God")

precious body emitting light from every orifice & hole, even the lowest backchannel: the gutters that ring the streets, the beautiful concave divot in each side of your ass, the places I tend with my mouth—precious body I absorb your refuse, spin your sins, your suit of shining beads, your coat of hesitation (o hesitate!) I didn't & what I did I don't regret (but) precious body I plunge my finger into your ellipses, I sink my teeth on your clavicle, I lick untold wreckages of nothing's changed & everything when you say do that & that & that "They took the stitches out & you could see the cut" (overheard in the restaurant) "Didn't you get head here once?" (overheard in the station) the trains enter the tunnels then exit & when you leave the hotel in the morning & when I leave the hotel in the morning the driver takes me faster to the wrong location & I ask the women in conversation beside the tracks which side to the city—precious body we've bought our tickets from the machine before boarding, we are throttling like a projector showing the film with the white bed that doesn't belong to us, our bodies entwined & moving faster than they have in years: the screen is rising, the motor is quieting, we are going under the river, precious body & I am tearing the screen & crumpling it up—I am stuffing all this inside me & when I open my mouth, my legs, my cunt, can you see the light— the everlasting & brilliant light that shoots out?

Are You Popular? (1947)

The missing woman's body—a girl, really—
    she was 22—*yoo hoo*—her body

sat in the Salinas Walmart Parking lot
    in her Volkswagen Jetta for months

before anyone noticed. Even the store
    security camera turned a blind eye

to the unmoving car. What makes anyone
    seen? Something to do with the lunchroom?

Something to do with parking in cars
    with boys at night? Each tray holds

a small carton of milk, diamond-shaped
    spout ripped open. Popularity—

what substance? What circle? Black holes.
    Torn mouths. Space itself responds

to the presence of matter by curving—
    by expanding or contracting. A needle.

A note. Her body in that car. She's a swell kid.
    Did you know her? I wish I did. She always

looked nice. She dated all the boys so they felt
    less important. Why do we care

how they felt? Because they enact violence.
    They fill holes. *Do you have your key, dear?*

She puts on her mittens. *I'll take good care of her,*
         he says, to reassure them. Black holes are

an exit door from the universe through which
         anything that passes can never return.

Where does she fit in all this? She thinks she's
         a very last resort. The sound of two

black holes colliding a billion light years away:
         water into a pool of more water,

wet darkness, the caves of their mouths?
         Girls who park in cars are not really

popular. Not even with the boys they park with.
         Not when they meet at school or elsewhere.

Not when space itself responds to the presence
         of matter in no discernible way. The vehicle

had tinted windows, a sunshade, didn't appear
         out of the ordinary. None of the employees

noticed though it sat unmoving for months—
         like a ringing black phone beside a chair

and the boys calling, calling.

Beyond Which

The Irish photographer at the cocktail party I crashed
had a small camera over his shoulder like a compact purse
and gave me his card which pointed me toward his website

where the portrait section was filled with women, small-
breasted, naked, looking pointedly at the camera or him or
both, smiling in their eyes but not their lips, unashamed

of their bodies, their breasts, their cunts, though the word
cunt or even *pussy* sounds too violent for his artistic pictures,
the models' furred triangles sometimes obscured by hands

or folds of sheets. The camera captures forms without
judgment—with light and an open shutter—with shadow
and bent angles, the exact way a specific body part

(curved elbow, erect cock, hollowed collarbone) catches
time to repeat in image: a hook snagging a thread, pulling
until we unravel into a new form—not reduced, but changed—

a place beyond which—a trace, exalted. Beyond which
is a place I would not go, but I went because you asked.
Because you asked, I sent low-res dioramas of body

and bedroom, selfies encased in windowsill sun,
each message another part of me, another lit band
of flesh, the way one might capture every space

in an open-plan house from different angles before
a broker puts it on the market. We part with everything
eventually, though some things return to us unbidden.

There is a disconnect, surely, between past and present
but I don't see it. If someone else looked at a photo
from now, and another from back then, they might say

we've done some hard living and that would be accurate.
The only image that's the same in these photos you've sent,
I've sent, is our ink: the skin drinks what it needs, swallows

lines and whole bodies in an attempt to fill the hole
left by what? A city sidewalk sometimes glitters
in the dark or is pockmarked with gum black as tar,

broken by delicate fissures running the length
of the block. This is the crack we fall into where time
holds its breath under water for the full expanse

of the murky East River. Should I tell you about
my rib cage? How it's expanded with age and love
to cradle my enormous, porous heart? When I confess

that my body is shifty, you say you want to lick
every shifting inch, which is lovely, but what I mean
is that my body is formless, terra nullius,

a permeable membrane, a moon palace—
and beyond which is the place we remain,
folding and unfolding together like a flower,

a pocket knife, a tangled heap of film when
we still used film, pulled from the canister,
felt—emulsive—skinlike—exposed (to the light).

Letter to Hillary on the Radical Hospitality of the Body

I want to tell you something about the body, though I'm not sure how to articulate it exactly. I've been trying all morning to write a meditation on the sensory, on touch, delineate between kinesthetic and haptic, and instead I am staring at the white hard-boiled egg I took from breakfast rolled on its side on my white desk. Instead, I am fielding texts from my sister who had a baby last week and says she has uncontrollable chills and wonders if this is normal hormonal postpartum stuff or what. I don't know the answer so I tell her to call her doctor in case it's an infection because it's Sunday and I'm at an artists' colony with period cramps and a slight hangover since last night a painter opened the massive barn where they keep sculptures-in-process, put some beer on ice, rigged up his phone, and threw a dance party where we did our best to lose ourselves in darkness and summer and Saturday night, Kendrick Lamar and Nicki Minaj, Kanye and even Aretha until our bodies stopped thinking of themselves at all and we were only movement—limbs pressing through air, helicopters, drummers, wind-up contraptions, turbine engines. Until we were all sweating profusely, taking turns standing in front of the lone fan, flapping our shirts up and out to let the generated wind cool skin we'd normally keep covered up. Outside the doors, split open to the rafters, there were fireflies pulsing mating codes, stars pushing forward their fused light, clouds trailing their dust across the face of the moon. Like them, we leave traces behind—of hair and skin, accumulations of bodily excess donated back to the earth, a measure of time and breath, like spit and blood and cum and piss. I have let so many things and people enter and sometimes inhabit my body for lengths of time, they're uncountable, and I'm sure you have too despite the fact that the world tells us as women to stay vigilant and shut. This is not about void or gap or hole, what's missing or punched through or needs filling. Yesterday on the way here I passed two storefronts in the same strip mall—Big Boyz Guns & Ammo next to Serenity Counseling Center, and then near the Sheetz a hiker walking the shoulder of 460 carrying a giant wooden cross that was at least half the size of himself. This is where I'd insert something about violence and mindfulness, grace and perhaps suffering, but who knows why anyone carries anything around until it gets so heavy we set it down. Hillary, this isn't working; I don't know any more about the body than I did to begin with except that I was surprised I still remember how to dance with abandon—it had been years. We carry our movements, muscle memory, scars of all kinds inscribed on our skin, and inside us a space-time continuum that contains all the people and places we've touched and tasted and walked through and dwelled in, and as soon as we move through them they change and vanish so I will open myself again and again. What I'm trying to say in this small body of a poem is that our bodies themselves are without regrets—persistent and mortal and relentless.

Invitation to Tender

My friend Danielle tells me
to use a slightly more capacious
we in my poems & I look up
capacious: ample, roomy, vast,

immense & think of the church
marquee across from Publix:
God is real & loves you since
the *you* is all of us & we don't

deserve this enormous Earth.
Along the beach here people
walk the wrack line, heads
bowed or plant themselves

on their knees in one spot
searching for washed-up
shark teeth in the shell hash.
Our configurations of attention

are sometimes surprising—
is it capitalism or adoration
that tells us we can inhabit
anything? There are many

ways to participate in
(egress from?) this world.
See the molten sun dropping
into the Gulf? The lightning

in the distance blinking the
clouds, trying to warn us?
There are still loggerhead
nests roped off with tri-

angulated wood stakes &
orange caution tape though
just today the Endangered
Species Act was weakened

to clear the way for mining
& drilling & development.
Every day at dawn volunteers
walk the beach to count

hatchlings, release any left
behind into the Gulf so they
don't get eaten by predators.
If there is an invitation to

tender it is written in drift
toys & sea glass—dunnage
swept in by the tide & left
right at our feet. We can all

procure. We can all excavate.
We can all strip down to our
softest parts & (satisfy the
client) make our best offer.

the bureau of reclamation

we the loyal companions
we who are hyped about everything
we who cross the thresholds of accountability
our songs of praise sound like gunshots
we the supermarket shoppers
we the leggings-as-pants wearers
we the shade throwers
the riven in nostalgia itinerants
who avoid our mail at all costs
who remember all our exes unequivocally
we the hypervigilant
we who collect regular explanations of benefits
we who worry about food security
we the invasive species
we who dwell (mostly) in the body
we who buried our long-suffering ancestors
what would you like to cup in your hands again?
water? a flame?
we the doom-scrollers
we who own wildlife patrol cameras
we the rendered who keep rendering
Louise Bourgeois once said I can express myself only in a desperate fighting position
we who want approval or adoration
we who see photographs as contraband
the neighbor captures a bear on film ambling through his yard
he warns the rest of us by posting the video on Facebook
we who see photographs as gestures
we the night texters
we who see photographs as certificates of presence
my grandmother received reparations from the German government
this was for performing slave labor during the war
we who believe god is (not) a consuming fire

blessed is the spectrum
i am paying attention
we the delicate or empty
we the toughened and leathery
we who are bound with floss to anything proximate
we the fruit skins stitched back together after they've been peeled down
we who know the difference between chemistry and alchemy
my children's expired passports
the dream about the boat
we who gather the exiles

This Volatile Taxonomy

(after Yve-Alain Bois & Rosalind Krauss)

the categories we locate
ourselves in are porous:
pulse / horizontality / base
materialism / entropy—
            the infinite un-
speakableness of the body
written in blood, excreta,
mucous membranes, pubic
hair: this type of alteration
(I am spotting) (I am unsure
of my direction) (I look at
my phone often) there is
no question of exhaustive-
ness (but we are exhausted
since) there are bodies that
have come from our bodies
& depend on (our bodies)
what is the answer to the un-
asked questions / there are
so many of them (something
we can find in lost space)
(something tucked) some-
thing parallel (my head
beneath yr arm & resting
on yr chest) the impassability
of the body's own frontier
(skin's the limit—& then)
(when you enter me) a line
or border separating two
countries (beyond which
lies wilderness) I am the un-

tamed thing, the weed or
rendering: but how could
we have presented [a happening]
without casting it in concrete?
how could we have shown
[an infinite overproduction]
without instantly betraying
or limiting it? (we are parents)
(we have lost so many things)

A Temple of the Spirit

Let's say you are on a plane, and before
the plane rises to clear congregations of
treetops and blue-gray mountains,
you watch the woman who called you up
by zone number then scanned your ticket—
you watch her from your plane seat don
a knit cap & head out to the runway to
wave your plane from the gate with two
bright orange batons, her arms held in an
uppercase L as our plane taxis past her
and her fluorescent green safety vest
to rise quickly over the tiny houses and
iced-over cattle ponds of the Eastern Shore.
Let's say that now you are on that plane
thrusting itself deep into clouds which
enshroud everything for a moment in a
dense halo of whiteness that is not fog—
the kind of bright cloudiness you'd expect
from the transition to a movie's dream
sequence or the opening to an episode
of *Highway to Heaven* with Michael Landon
right before he walks down that deserted
canyon road, duffel bag in hand, then hops
in a baby blue 1977 Ford when Victor French
pulls over for him. In the show, Landon is
actually an angel stripped of his wings.
He and French (a retired cop) are given
assignments by The Boss to help troubled
humans overcome their problems. What I'm
saying is sometimes we are asked to arrive
in a new city and assume the identities of
business employees or civil service workers

for the greater good. Or sometimes we are forced
to hold out our arms like cheerleaders for a team
we don't believe in as if our bodies can influence
the score no matter what we are thinking, but
what if the team is humanity? I don't know
if there's a god, but sometimes we are asked
to carry a baton for long periods of time as if
we're in a relay and can hand it off to the
next person waiting usually somewhere other
than the place we began, though that action is
so tricky and fails often. I hope the gate woman
was L for team Lift-off or Levity or Love of the
human race—Luck for our tin can with twin
engines newly cleared of snow. Let's say yes.

All the Secrets and Holes

The student project box in the library
above the book drop reads "I need 1000
secrets for an art project—Place Your
Secrets Here" and my friend Johnny says
nice try FBI—I'm not falling for that
again as we pass by and he's from
New Zealand, foreign but in a way
(white) that means he won't be asked
for his papers which all foreigners
on campus are now required to carry
since the inauguration and next to the
box is a coffee tin labeled "Hole Punches"
and it's not clear why someone would
be collecting small holes, detritus,
negative space made manifest.
Tonight I watched my neighbors
assemble a trampoline in their yard
with other neighbors. It was kind of
like an Amish barn raising if barns
came in boxes from Walmart and
the Amish drank beer from bottles
wrapped in bright neoprene koozies.
One neighbor was there wearing
sunglasses at dusk to hide her still-
swollen eyes as she just put her dog
down (cancer) and everyone could
see that dog was in pain except my
neighbor who was inured to the fact
that he was limping along, that the tumor
was growing so fast one of his eyes
looked noticeably different. I contain
1000 secrets, could fill that whole box

in the library myself. My neighbors
tell me their secrets too: the divorce
lawyer consult, the tween daughter
who got caught vaping pot in the
middle school bathroom, the husband
who isn't interested in sex anymore,
the crushing debt and second mortgage.
But the trampoline is almost done—
winched together with bolts and
zip ties, a black hole in the yard
the kids will use to launch themselves
toward the sky at dusk, contrails
crossing the last bit of blue with Xs
before they dissipate.

Now That I Can See the Light

I keep trying to write a poem and all I've got are some photos on my iPhone
(I can't stop taking them) through the chain-link safety fence of the building

they're pulling down piece by piece outside my office—an old ROTC dorm
that's been reduced to a pile of rubble and tangled piping by a yellow demo-

lition excavator with concrete cutter jaws and this thing looks so much
like a pet dinosaur that I can't help but have some tender feelings

toward its pulverizing tendencies, the way it bends its head just so to
take a bite from the second-floor cinder blocks or reaches into an empty

window frame to grab a hunk of wires and pull as if it's unraveling a skein
of yarn, but the upshot is that after three weeks of walking past my colleagues'

windows and doing a double take because it looks like Beirut in the 80s or
Syria or Gaza or another locale in the Middle East, which are the only frame-

works any of us can think of to describe this derby—after three weeks, now
we've got a clear view of the Zaxby's and a McDonald's across the way.

I went to the state liquor store for a bottle of fancy rum to gift my friend Matt
on his 40th birthday and the girl working the register was wearing a name tag:

Bryanna / Spirit Guide, I swear to god, and I was hopeful. She didn't know
much about rum, but told me the name of the artist one town over who carved

the entirely okay tattoo of a phrase in cursive on the inside of her wrist. I didn't
read what it actually said because I was too distracted by the clarity of the letters,

their tails and swirls. I don't remember the last time someone licked that particular
place on my body—seriously, just touch the inside of your wrist lightly and think

about who's been there last—but I'm pretty sure it was some guy who was trying
to impress me probably years ago with his attention to sensuality because who still

tries now that we're over 40? That building: falling dust, and sky framed in window
casings hanging on through the slow dissembling. One day when the machine

started on the dorm's internal hallways: a mural astronaut's hand reaching toward
"the eternal pursuit of perfection" in painted script while a whole drawing class sat

outside on the stoop across from it trying to render the demolition (erasure?)
in pencil. That building became a metaphor for everything: my body, in bone-

crunching pain every time I sit down because of my SI joints or pelvis or whatever
is no longer holding my spine together correctly; my week at work, everything

a near-catastrophe punctuated by pulverized plaster, doorways collapsing,
wires sprouting from the stripped walls like exasperation, which is to say

that I've got a case of the Mondays or it's hump day or TGIF we all head
past the dust to the Appalachian beer garden on a farm where our children

run feral in giant piles of mulch & the adults drink-talk in clumps into dusk
the third night of fall which is something like an overturned plastic wagon

missing a wheel in a field of browned sunflowers. We've worn summer / our
bodies / our buildings, out almost nearly entirely with long-ago joy but what

I want to tell you is that even this dissembling is beautiful, disarming, familiar
when I run my own fingers over the tender veins on the inside of my wrist.

Swift Trucks

This place has views

of black cows, heads bent,
some galloping across a field.

That's from the left side.

To the right, there's the runaway
truck ramp on I-85, rutted

and eschewing abandon.

What isn't stuck somewhere
godforsaken? Only

one of these statements

is true and you get to pick:
he wants to have a word

with us or I can't pay

for gas no more. O Country
View Motel. I press

the shutter release and say

yes to the sound of your
(captured) face, to fists

made of facts, to whatever

doesn't pay the rent but
means well anyway.

This is not the poem

in which someone invented
the term hypnotism.

In which you say yes

to what you see—yes,
we must get it seen to.

Only one of these

statements are true:
your face carries

a certain strangeness

that does not surface
much or your photos

(when threaded together

like jewels) bear every
message you were excited by

when the world spoke to us.

When the world spoke to you
it said stay. It said fragmentary.

It touched your face, your

beleaguered tender important face
and said this and this and this.

Ghost Eden

(after Anthony Haughey's "Settlement")

Garden of rock.
Garden of brick and heather.
        Garden of cranes with their hands raised
as if they know the yellow answer:
        to gather together—safety in numbers.
Garden of drywall frames, holes for windows
        punched out like teeth. Garden of bar fights.
Garden of rubble and gaps,
        spectral for-sale signs knocked
from wooden posts, bleached down
        to numbers ending in gardens of overgrown lots.
We are falling into ruin, garden
        of scaffolding and shale and gravel—
give us back our peace: a half-built garden
        of theft, treasures hidden in darkness,
newspapers crumpled on subfloors telling us
        to hold fast to that which is good.
Garden of rebar and saplings with trunks
        encased in corrugated piping
because many animals can girdle
        a tree's bark quickly: deer, stray cats, rabbits.
Garden of Tyvek wrap loosed
        and flapping like a ship's sail
in the gales, in the sheeting storms.
        Hanging laundry left out in the garden
past darkness, fruit from the tree
        of humanness: socks, shirts, underpants.

Garden of long exposures, half-light, traces
        that empty themselves in tire treads running
like ladders through red clay mud:
        the dirt from which we are formed
and crushed and formed again.

Missing Parts

Hillary, I'm sorry about yr friend who killed himself—sometimes
this world is too much to hold inside us or move through

We pass a place called Crystal Cave and now Endless Caverns
as if we're meant to be subterranean or sheltered in this storm
or always   I've been spelunking

only once for real and at various points had to squeeze myself
through slick clay passages so narrow they felt like birth canals
and my friend Kate had to take an emergency Xanax in the darkness
before we turned back toward the cave's mouth

We've been driving through the clouds hanging low over Mauzy
and Broadway and Timberville and every town on 81 for hours
in the dark and rain and I am not absent from this car

I am here   I am silent lost in thought writing to you with a
husband driving & two sons in the back   Are they

mine or just proximate?   How or why do we claim anyone?
In yr last letter you asked me   *What if I can't accept my own happiness?*

and I consider this when my son asks *How many satellites
are in the sky and how do people get them up there so easily?*
I think the answer is rockets

I understand the wish to have yr body turned to ashes & dust
then scattered on water or wind or even shot into space

I do not know where I want to rest when I'm gone since
I don't feel at home anywhere except some subway platforms
and when I'm in motion passing through corridors or terminals

Some days I think I've got a missing part—the satellite
that handles contentment which is a lot like happiness
which is the opposite of crisis

I am excellent in most emergencies but restless when I am with
my family in the car singing along to "Purple Rain" or even when
everyone is asleep in the backseat and it's quiet except for
asphalt humming under our tires like radio static

The accumulation of dust is a kind of physical index
for the passage of time but to accumulate anything
in a fine coating you need to not-move

you need to be very still like a photograph of yrself
but even those are live now   you can keep

a small fluttering on yr phone—the essence
of someone   we pass fireworks   nude girls

things outlawed then un-   depending on state lines
we travel bodies of bridges stretched over water
the hometown of an old lover   I still remember

his hipbones beneath mine and the way he drew me
a map of this exact highway with the birthplace
of Eugene O'Neill labeled in purple marker

O Connecticut, you are an endless radar on the
interstate median tracking our speed   my youngest
asking if we've put the wrong place into the GPS

I have lived what feels like many restless lives in this
one body   *Keep going—You didn't fail at quitting*

You just haven't finished the process says a billboard
talking about smoking but maybe it could also pertain
to happiness   we are in-process   we are trying

so hard and the rain—we can barely see through
the windshield   the rain, it won't let up

An Occupation of Loss

(The Pink House, 9325 North Bayshore Drive)

If this place has a secret spatial heart,
I can't see it. Its want and shame are
protected by layers of concrete, gray
and white patches mottling the famous
bright rose and salmon stucco façade.
The house is a machine for living in,

wrote Le Corbusier, and this one has
a bias toward wetness, puts forth
pink on water as risqué contrast—
hues of our most intimate chambers:
flamingo feathers and delicate conch-
shell innards layered in planes. Water

unravels memory, erases claims to
body and time and space. What if
you said *open up for me*, and you didn't
mean my mouth. In the original
sketches by Laurinda Spear, the house
is cerulean, glows from within, casts

its shadow out at night into Biscayne Bay
and is also surrounded by it—as if the house
is simultaneously subaqueous and floating,
stairs descending into liquid at either end.
In one drawing, a sailboat named Eurydice
is moored to a banister, while a lone

woman in a one-shouldered gown stands
on an inset balcony looking out blankly
to the flat azure horizon, echoing every

upscale condo brochure. This is not
museum-quality luxury, or a world-class
lifestyle of signature amenities. In the myth,

when Orpheus looks back, a city doesn't
burn from iniquity; a city doesn't turn to salt—
but his heart. At the entrance of the house,
an aqua porthole to the pool: a single
blue eye weeping, a peephole, a camera's
lens, the unnerving beauty of perforations.

A photograph is a writing of light, a witness
that fixes structures in a moment. And maybe
the architect knew we were anticipating what
would inevitably come besides renovation, flood,
cataclysm, or demolition—the slow wearing-down
of splendor and sometimes desire. When you left

and went radio silent I thought of you saying
I'm always tempted to just walk into the ocean.
And yet, sketched in the corners in faint pencil
on the front of the house plans that weren't
quite blueprint: *Miami Night*—and on the back,
I will wait for you.

A Brief Ontological Investigation

What can I say to cheer you up? This afternoon the sky is like five portholes between the clouds. The unidentifiable weeds are tall and still unidentifiable and I miss the cows in the field, where have they gone? Sometimes one would wander then stand in the middle of the road and I'd have to stop my car and wait for it to decide to finish crossing. I am drinking seltzer through a straw because of my injury and I have inexplicable bruises on the side of my thigh and I just spent the last five minutes watching a bird through my window sitting in the small crotch where two phone lines x together though it flew off before I could take a picture of it. In the urgent care waiting room this morning there was a magazine with a proven neuroscience article on rituals that will make us happy and the first was practicing gratitude but when I tried to think of something right there next to the guy with the walker and the woman with gauze held to her cheek I came up blank. Because I am a terrible person I will tell you that my favorite neighbor does this thing I hate with her kids called heart-bread, where they're forced each night before bed to go around one by one and come up with a moment of gratitude and I want to tell her that we can thank anything—the crushed cans in recycling, my wristwatch for keeping time, the rainstorm yesterday that had water pouring from the gutters. I mean, we all overflow; we all feel an abundance of something but sometimes it's just emptiness: vacant page, busy signal, radio static, implacable repeat rut where the tone arm reaches across a spinning vinyl record to play it again, rest its delicate needle in a groove and caress forever the same sound from the same body. Which is to say that the opposite of ennui is excitement and I'm not feeling it either today even a little. Not in the CVS while browsing the shiny electric rainbow nail polish display indefinitely while waiting for my prescription. And probably not on my run later no matter how bucolic the mountains seem in the 5 p.m. heat. The second ritual in that article was to touch people, which is easy if you're with people you can touch but I'm in too loud a solitude and can only touch myself which reminds me of that old Divinyls song and I'm pretty sure that's not what the article meant. Buber says *you has no borders* but he's talking about god I think since this is not true of us because we all have bodies which make us small countries or maybe islands. If summer means our bodies are more porous perhaps we're also more open to this inexplicable sadness that hangs here from the cinder blocks, drags itself across the barbed-wire fence. What I'm trying to tell you is that I'm not cheered up either. That bird, before it flew off, I like to think of the crossed wires, the impenetrable conversations rushing under its feet.

The Practice of Depicting Matter as It Passes from Radiance to Decomposition

Last night I saw horses in a gated pasture at dusk

It was still over 100 degrees though it was darkening

We live in public

When we pass next to water it glitters with movement and light

This can induce melancholy

I revisit all the bits of my past I can't shake but it's not nostalgia, just the porous borders of summer

I was walking, I was slick with sweat then gritty with salt

We think we have many homes, but our only home is the body—these space-time machines, these sculptures of fluid and rind and scaffolding, of breath and membrane and pleasure

How far can your arm reach when you stretch it in front of you?

This is the Theory of the Very Near

We are like turntables—delicate stylus coaxing sound from a rotating body, sometimes the same song on repeat for years

This is what it means to get into the groove

Rivers of stitch and valleys of bone

Sometimes the bodies are those of others, or sometimes our own

Lately I think more about where I'd like my body to rest

What I'm saying is we are all in this together, this accrual of scars, this palace of objects

What I'm saying is grasp something tightly, then let it drop

We slough off everything, starting with our hair and skin

Which becomes dust, an index of time and accumulation

letter from around the way

if I tried to describe this neighborhood (to you—
always to you) it would be driveway basketball
hoop after driveway basketball hoop, all of them
set to different heights for the kids who toss
every object to the sky to see what comes back
down (gravity) and what falls through the net
(skill or dumb luck) with a swish-crack-crack

it's golden hour, and at the bottom of the hill
two neighbors I don't know share a drink
on a gray deck together while all at once
the redbud blossom like a dress with many
holes (my bare shoulders, the small of my
back, I can feel your breath brushing all
the places) the tulips are almost blooming

like pursed lips or hands with fingers pushed
together (to enter where?) when you enter
me it's nothing like I remember—softer
and more porous, the wings of your hipbones
invisible now under flesh since you are heavy
with the weight of adulthood and I am also
marked with the raised scars of every thing

that passed through me and also loss but this
is not how I see us when we are spooning (you
tucked deep in me and wrapped around every
part) I don't know myself these days and I don't
know you much now either but what returns
to us what boomerangs back what we inhabit
again and again becomes a home of kinds

an axis of memory that helps us position our-
selves make alliance with things that are not
our bodies at the top of the hill one neighbor's
son stands at the edge of a curbside drainage
ditch balancing on one foot then the other
and you are up late sketching squared off
rooms the unlit plans of mansions for one per-

centers grand palaces neither of us will ever
live in we live in the palace of the body the
place we disappear once and once more
our shining skins and entryways welcoming
whatever knocks or brushes up against us
the lights at dusk coming on one by one in
each house the windows gaping and lit

Message from the Interior

(after Walker Evans)

There are so many you's inside of me

Soft structures of tentative conjectures

Or the myth of linear progress

Where a you + an I grow closer

Through the architecture of information

Until we are a congregation of night texters

Certain shapes bind us together

Think topology: geometrical properties + spatial relations

Constituent parts or

Tensile strength—something pulling something else

First I felt adored / then I felt complicit

You + I are directly related to one another in community

Triangulation: I am addressing ~~a beloved~~ an audience

We are part of a [public] ceremony

The underlying concerns of virtual intimacy

Into the humid inclination our uncurbed suspicion

Whatever is happening keeps happening

Think desire lines: the shortest route between

An origin (I) + a destination (you)

When they do not fade, or until they fade

You are every room of this dwelling

You can stay here as long as you like

Smith Street, 1998

your eyes were like a fire door or submarine hatch, and tell me again

how you want me to leave from a room in a way that's not ghosting,

that marks presence and brings back artifacts from ocean shipwrecks

with scuba suits: the ones in museums with metal helmets and glass

visors because the men—all the men who wore them, who were inside

of them, of me, of the holy deep, in the space between entering and

staying, because the leaving the cities it was always the keys tossed

in a bowl on the table the chain sliding the lock in the doorways of

buildings with stairways to climb the moving into the neighbors'

cooking or yelling or fucking no matter the hallway your hands

and the space between filled with my body my body my body not

exactly fading but peacemaking but gravity but colorless but rain

and even the rain saying how connected we are with everyone how

iced over how january—*the space of everyone that has just been inside*

of everyone mixing

What Follows Is a Reconstruction Based on the Best Available Evidence

1. I ate eggs from a chafing dish while the baker reminded us: *the only thing that will hurt you out here are your own bad decisions*

2. I felt fettered then un-

3. I listened to the rain

4. I listened to the rain hitting the Carrier compressor, the gravel walk

5. I listened to the rain flattening the clover, I listened to the rain letting up and then it was ozone and drip

6. On the bench under the overhang in the rain I let myself pretend I was younger and childless, like the first time I arrived here

7. The first time I arrived here, I never thought *I am small and luminous*

8. The body, burdened and miraculous

9. The body as thin-nest boundary

10. I climbed into your body like a cave

11. I was frightened to walk in the dark

12. Late at night even my own movements became unknowable, magnified and rustling

13. The night cut by the moon, punctured by the whistle of the cargo train

14. There was only a hole, there was only forward and more forward

15.   The inevitability of a scarred life, your pulse, stitches, this palace
      of breath

16.   go on, go on / again, again / return, return

we used to go to the Bulgarian Bar but not together

(for D.)

the place on Broadway & Canal whose motto
was *helping ugly people have sex since 416 BC* and
it probably had another name but everyone
only knew it as the Bulgarian Bar where
Gogol Bordello frontman Eugene Hutz
who was sexy in that sweaty limber way like
Mick Jagger but much skeezier & with a thick
Ukrainian accent DJ'ed Gypsy music & we
figured this out somehow while reminiscing
about our 20s in NYC via text & our 20s
in the city were PowerPoint temp jobs were
stealing rolls of toilet paper from restaurant
bathrooms were pagers & flip phones & pay
phones were July subway platform infernos
were whiffs of hot copper & pee & trash
were walkup cockroaches were dive bar
makeout sessions were chain-smoking on
fire escapes & unspecified parades rolling
past tall office windows were brick façade
or window casements falling to the sidewalk
& shattering at our feet were illegal sublets
& late rent checks & spit-shined heartbreak
when nothing & nobody depended on us &
she said, *Did I tell you I head-butted a girl*
in the face there one night dancing?
Not on purpose but still . . .

The Replication Machine

Hillary, I miss taxis at night—do people still use them, or is it all Uber and Lyft?

The way their yellow bodies shush down Houston or Broadway especially in the rain and you raise your hand and there's one sidling up next to you open and ready to take you nowhere predetermined with their lighted hats of ads perched jauntily on top at your service

I also miss my unlimited MetroCard, though pushing through turnstiles with my hips never had the same slick cachet as sliding across a backseat then telling the driver an intersection, and was often hard to swipe when drunk, but I loved its lack of accountability and the fact that my final destination was a mystery sometimes even to me

In "The Work of Art in the Age of Mechanical Reproduction" Walter Benjamin talks about Eugène Atget's photos of deserted Paris streets—that he photographed them like scenes of crimes, for the purpose of establishing evidence

I'm positive the whole alcohol-soaked photographic tour you sent me last night of your walk from the Lower East Side to the West Village was not a crime, but I loved seeing that woman in the tight white cocktail dress and heels in a fluorescent pizza parlor eating a slice standing up from here in my perch in the Blue Ridge mountains at 1 a.m.

And I also loved the animated red-headed dude in the cheetah print overalls with no shirt underneath talking to you in the video with no sound

The photo of the Weed World truck parked on the corner of Bleecker and Lafayette

The pic of you with your THC lollipop

I'm going to say this though it makes me sound old AF: back before Y2K we didn't have this technology (obviously)

The best evidence we could gather from a hard night of drinking was a body next to us in the morning (or not)

"The city is a huge monastery," said Erasmus

There's the corner of Washington Square, Broadway and Mercer, the Water-Soda-Chicken-Kebab-Hot-Dog-Truck on video playing street music I can't name in a language I can't decipher—maybe Arabic disco or Spanish rap

In the last frame you sent, tail and brake lights of cabs shine extra bright with halos flaring red as lips or emergency flashers, a cluster of want and accidents

An aura is a *unique phenomenon of distance* (Benjamin again)

You are far away and I am a beholder—one who beholds

We all have a desire to bring things closer

The photo leaves its locale to be received in the studio of a friend, a lover, a stranger, whomever

Don't we all have auras / halos / glares that obscure the thing beneath, our outlines and shapes

Don't we all have imperceptible apertures where the light gets in

Welcome to Fear City: A Survival Guide

the memory where my grandmother is a light-filled hole, where she takes me on the subway (blue E? orange F?) from Forest Hills–Continental–71st Avenue she is holding my hand on the platform (gray, pockmarked with black gum and green girders, yellow rumble strip with raised bumps warning us before the tracks) it is 1979 and I am in a coat (navy wool with toggle buttons) and the light in the station is pulled through the grate above us like thread through the eye of a needle though it's impossible as the station was deeper underground than I remember so that light must have come from somewhere my grandmother with her coiffed helmet of jet black hair we were going to her office (why? I'm not sure) she worked in a showroom with bolts and bolts of fabric (an upholstery shop?) and on the platform before the silver train came there was a woman who was totally bald, her head shining in the pulled-in light and I want to say she was wearing a fox-fur coat but I'm sure that's not right she was luminous and unashamed and tall but all adults were though maybe not my grandmother who was vain and stayed out of the sun and was (frankly) unpleasant not warm or beloved and when we were together we were usually silent unless she was instructing me in her clipped Czech accent the last time I saw her alive in the time right before death (there's a name for this space) when people get truer than usual lose their filter start saying things they normally wouldn't and she pulled me to her white folded nursing home cot to warn me (I can't remember the exact words) about not being sexually cold or frigid about making sure I had sex with my husband with someone because she had stopped and closed up shop long ago rolled desire up like a bolt of fabric the upshot was to stay open to pleasure to provide pleasure to accept pleasure and I listened to her never didn't listen through invasive technology sutures boredom whatever came my way I grew up in Fear City where we tucked our necklaces in our shirts on the streets rode the subway in daytime only kept extra tokens laced into our sneakers heard hands up motherfuckers more than once knew at any moment on the sidewalk where bodies were in relation to ours this hypervigilant radar someone always flashing dick pissing against the side of a brick building but the city was always glittering at night even through the windows of a locked Oldsmobile Cutlass Ciera cruising a bridge rusting into the East River grandmother the light I am still going toward it

The Last Decade of the 20th Century

That's when bar napkins in Brooklyn were interesting,
When answering machine messages meant something
More than an emoji of an eggplant or a peach. This has
Nothing to do with baba ghanouj or the local Lebanese
Place that closed because it's so hard to find help these
Days in the kitchen. My friend Nadine sent me Orange
Blossom Water from Beirut for my insomnia but it didn't
Work like it should have. It kept me up all night instead
Texting you fragments of poems that were actually an
Inventory of garage sale items. A gold plastic participant
Trophy. A snow globe from a place I didn't want to visit
To begin with. The sound of a voice clicking and clicking,
A squiggling rewind. Remember these things? I would like
To visit with you in the way people did in the 19th century,

With calling cards and polite conversation in the parlor.
I would like to discuss theory or what the neighbors are
Up to on their gated estates. Then we might adjourn to
Somewhere less upright and label all the family heirlooms
With sticky tags. Then we might hock everything for armfuls
Of golden Sacagawea dollars and run off in a pickup with
A king cab. I promise to stay strapped in and stick to my
Side of the bench seat with sweat pooling under my thighs.
We can head to the nearest Sheetz for egg sandwiches
And American Spirits. We can determine nothing is cause
For alarm or impropriety. You can tell me about the magic
Of summer, the patterns glitter makes when you use it
To outline a body on the sidewalk instead of chalk. Then
The body gets up, walks away from its own negative space,
Change jangling in its lucky pockets.

Come Correct

If my lips are zipped—if I keep our delicious and contagious secret
—if I am amnesiac or too hungover to remember your mouth

on mine—if I forget the imprint of your body indelibly stamped—
if I search for you, call for you, lover, stranger, alien—if I offer up

gratitude to the air—if I rob you of your signals and energy (are you
battery-powered?)—if we fuck again and again all scorching night—

if we lock our power up to prevent a meltdown—if we twine ourselves
together like an interrobang—if we cross the imperial sea holding hands

or recycle our bodies into danger zones—if we do not yield—if I let you
come deep inside me (finally)—if we buy more time—if your body is a

snow-covered mountain—if your body is an emergency—if you sing
karaoke (I Will Survive? The Boxer?) under the stage lights at Tokyo Rose—

if our bodies become facsimiles or ghosts of themselves, like melted
snow or animal tracks—if you leave me—I need to say this, so listen:

if you go, do it quickly—the way a rabbit darts into the brush

Remember Me as a Time of Day

heartbreak is a fixture of the landscape
like these unbuttoned doors, these streetlamps
over bent pavement, glittering, emitting heat

with covers pushed to the floor there is nothing
lonelier than an air conditioning unit (5,000 BTUs)
or a chain lock and the space between the door

and the frame ~~heartbreak~~
is so steep you don't really race up to it
those men ringing the buzzer (no soliciting)

a motion of crossing the street
(heartbreak) is imminent
against the window against the light

I want you here now with me
to do dangerous things:
salt flats, salt mines, diamonds since

heartbreak is the opposite of acrylic is
dawn over a bridge (rusted, impassable)
Carroll Street Verrazzano Kosciuszko

the river rises to the promenade
after heavy rains,
                    the bright sky

cooing into the night, flying home, roosting
like music in the Anchorage, like music
echoing everywhere we went

whether we stay or go
heartbreak is an option
Verrazzano himself was killed and eaten

by natives of Guadeloupe or executed
for piracy in Spain: heartbreak
is not always a linear progression

the experience we are thrust into

I am stuck at a middle school band concert where the conductor
is getting weepy about Jesus on the cross while announcing
the next song in the program—"Eloi, Eloi" which he first heard
performed post-tsunami by a Japanese orchestra, and before
the kids begin, the teacher-conductor butchers the Hebrew phrase
Jesus shouts at the ninth hour, which should be *eli, eli, lama azavtani*:
my god, my god, why have you forsaken me? and I'm wondering
about separation of church and state—this Jesus concert, which is
not unlike my 8-hour flight from Dublin last week where the Irish
man next to me headed to Arlington for training in computer coding
showed me his book about Mary Magdalene, told me about his
conversion experience at Lourdes which involved his dead mother
and falling to his knees and weeping, then burning his books on
yoga and Buddhism, his heavy metal albums too. He was insistent
there is only one truth—that Jesus was the messiah and whatever
I said about Judaism was irrelevant. My discomfort was palpable,
and it wasn't just our cramped tray tables with their basic economy
pretzels. I wanted to tell him I was spilled like water too once,
but I did not find Jesus, wasn't even looking, though I did weep
on the plane next to him while watching *Crazy Rich Asians*.
I wanted to say we're all driven by desire and bodily experience,
and occasionally guilt, but instead I thought of the photo an ex
once sent me of himself in an airplane bathroom in a gray hoodie—
the one he wears, he said, so he can cry undisturbed on planes
because we are untethered and powerless at altitude, and often
we grope around for matter to breathe our spirit into. His face
was not in the photo; his zipper was halfway down exposing his
dick, which was out just over the sink like a conductor's wand,
or those satellite photos of an astronaut tethered off-ship and
about to float into space. To allow—to permit—to forgive—
to forsake—to abandon—each time I open my phone my heart
is like wax melting in my chest, a saint candle from a supermarket

shelf and the band is trying to play the theme song from *Mission Impossible* now—they're on their third start—the conductor is apologetic, but they can't get the rhythm right: 5/4 time and percussion didn't rehearse with winds due to class scheduling so the instruments sound like they're racing each other in a relay where someone keeps falling behind, has dropped the baton. We are failing each other in every possible arena, this auditorium of listeners, a metal tube throttling through clouds, the spectacle of love or crucifixion or vulnerability, a conversion experience at 40,000 feet. *Do you not know your bodies are temples of the holy spirit?* I think, each time I look at my phone glowing like a flame I cup in my hands.

Letter on Gratitude

Hillary, it's the night after Thanksgiving & everyone is asleep / I'm in the living room of my childhood home / my father has installed a timer that turns lights on automatically / the timer sounds like the fuse to a homemade bomb / my Chilean aunt made flan & Brazo de Reina for second Thanksgiving / an ex posts a shirtless photo of himself by a window / I wondered if he had a thanksgiving at all / the way the sunlight cut across his body / my sons were piled on their cousins watching *Teen Titans Go!* / my uncle is dying slowly / my sister's baby, we passed her around like a potato / when she cried we bounced from the knees / when she cried my mother made jokes about putting her up for adoption / told one cousin to have another child / told the other about my sister's 23 frozen eggs / forgot my cousins are infertile / forgot my son is adopted / I ate fruit & brownie pie & flan & Brazo de Reina / I helped clear the table / I listened to my mother's cousin talk about the war / she told us about a man with two dachshunds on the train with Uncle Jack to the DP camp at Bergen Belsen / she was an orphan by then / *the opera singer that met us at the Port Authority*, she said / *her nails were manicured & I was so impressed* / *the stupid things you remember*, she said / my sister made us go around to announce our gratitudes & I felt impossibly empty / I felt very still / I wanted to say *I had dim sum, I saw exhibits, I wandered the strangely deserted streets of Soho at night* / I said *my family*, but what I meant was *my desire* / when I was younger I thought I could return indefinitely / turn toward the body of the city always slightly unchanged somehow & waiting for me / late afternoon shadows splayed on the faces of buildings / in that golden light & traffic nothing needing me, my gratitude or praise

My List of True Facts

I am forty-three and I just drove to CVS at 9:30 p.m. on a Sunday
to buy a store-brand pregnancy test two sticks in a box
rung up by a clerk who looked like the human embodiment
of a Ken doll with his coiffed blond hair and red smock
even though I wished there was a tired older woman
at the register this once even though I am sure I am
not pregnant this missing my period is almost definitely
another trick of perimenopause along with the inexplicable
rage at all humans the insane sex drive and the blood that
when it comes overwhelms everything with two sons
already what would I do with a baby now even though
I spent four long years trying to have another I am done
have given away all the small clothes and plastic devices
that make noise just looking at toddlers leaves me exhausted
this would be a particularly cruel trick of nature the CVS
was empty there was no one in cosmetics or any aisle including
family planning which is mostly lube and condoms I didn't
know Naturalamb was a thing "real skin-to-skin intimacy"
there's just one small half of one shelf of pregnancy tests
and some say no/yes in case you don't think you can read
blue or pink lines appearing in a circle my grandmother
was a nurse-midwife during the war in the Sosnowiec ghetto
her brother ten years younger *a change-of-life child* she called him
when she told me finally she had a brother when the archivists
came around for her testimony years after her brother was gassed
alongside her mother in Auschwitz years after my grandmother
euthanized her own daughter whom I was named for because
the SS were tossing babies from the windows of cattle cars
change-of-life child the name for a baby born to an older mother
past forty I peed on so many sticks over so many years
gave myself scores of injections took pills went under anesthesia
and knives since there's an unspoken mandate to procreate

when all your people your family were actually slaughtered
I gave one son my grandmother's brother's name and
the other was called King Myson by his birth mother
on the page of notes we got that she filled out before she
gave him up it took me an hour of staring at the form
before I realized it was *my son* she was claiming him
before she let him go and I think the morning will bring
nothing just one blue line but right now it is still night
and I am sitting in my car under the parking lot lights
which are bright and static like me and beyond them
there's the clerk in the red smock locking the doors

Beyond Which

my seatbelt is fastened and
I no longer smoke and I want
to tell you everything since
we have history that predates
(~~precedes preexists~~) predawn

first I met an irish photographer
who did portraiture—the female
form: all women with exposed
breasts, a small camera tucked
under his arm, unferocious

second, it's been more than
twenty years since I stumbled
to your door at night where I was
always welcome with my current
state of nostalgia for what?
leaving in the morning, a city
sidewalk by itself is nothing—
an abstraction; it means something
only in conjunction with your
body folded into mine or mine
folded into yours or or or
  [insert more here]

third: from the window the edges
of a state (unidentifiable)—its
mottled blue waters, its shoreline
and archipelagos, its small lines
of boats—this is not the state
the plane is meant to hover above
so there's a landing (unscheduled)
in Baltimore to refuel

fourth, I was breathtaking
(or maybe you said beautiful)

fifth—what may happen decades
from now—beyond the imagined
event horizon—is not only un-
known but unknowable

sixth, the memory of our origin
has been lost and this is perhaps
true of everyone:

a hunk of lead pipe on a
gold chain or your hipbones
pulled toward me; seven
shudders and damages; your
virtuosity

eight: "in this painting you can
read a love letter to a headless
body whose lips are lovingly
described as *a coral reef in the surf* "
—the theme: unbridled passion—
materials and technique: oil, chicken-
wire, rope, textile on hardboard

nine happened so slowly and
to such an extent that I wasn't
even aware of change until one
day I decided to walk around
the block and found that we had
no block and then I decided to
walk around the neighborhood
and found that we had no
neighborhood—only the

entropy of bodies over time:
by accumulation; by infinite
profusion; by wear and tear

ten is we embrace
the hard and sweet dumbness
of the physical world—its
mute wreckage, the things that
vanish and vanish and vanish—
hush

Notes

The epigraphs for the book are taken from Walt Whitman's poem "To You," Gilles Deleuze and Félix Guattari's "Balance Sheet-Program for Desiring-Machines," and James Baldwin's "Introduction to Exhibition of Beauford Delaney, Opening December 4, 1964 at the Gallery Lambert."

"Seven Fragments About Christmas and an Episode of Night Swimming" contains some titles of books by photographer Edward Ruscha.

"Médium Adam 25" is the name of the synthetic resin binder that makes International Klein Blue a unique and intense paint color specific to Yves Klein.

The title "Eternity Now" comes from a sculpture by Sylvie Fleury that's displayed on the front of the Bass Museum of Art in Miami Beach.

"Elegy with Lo-Fi Selfie" is for Chris Ostoj (1974–2002).

Are You Popular? is a 1947 social hygiene film from the Prelinger Archives. The poem also references the death of a young woman who was found inside her car on February 3, 2016 by Walmart employees in Salinas, CA (as reported by KSBW and other news outlets).

"This Volatile Taxonomy" contains phrases from the book *Formless: A User's Guide* by Yve-Alain Bois and Rosalind Krauss (Zone Books, 1997).

The title "A Temple of the Spirit" comes from a 1943 letter to Frank Lloyd Wright, where the Guggenheim Museum's first director, Hilla Rebay, asked him to design "a temple of the spirit."

"Missing Parts" is for Hillary Adler. The line "The accumulation of dust is a kind of physical index for the passage of time" comes from the essay "Notes on the Index: Seventies Art in America" by art critic Rosalind Krauss.

"An Occupation of Loss" owes a debt to Alastair Gordon's "On Pinkness: The Pink House and Its Secret Spatial Heart" in *The Miami Rail* (24 June 2017).

"A Brief Ontological Investigation" has a line in it from *I and Thou* by Martin Buber, translated by Walter Kaufman (Touchstone, 1970).

The title "The Practice of Depicting Matter as It Passes from Radiance to Decomposition" comes from a line in Olivia Laing's book *The Lonely City: Adventures in the Art of Being Alone* (Picador, 2016) about the work of artist Zoe Leonard.

The title "Message from the Interior" comes from a book of photographs by Walker Evans of the same name, originally published in 1966 by Eakins Press. The line "When they do not fade, or until they fade" comes from Erika Luckert, cited in Ellie Violet Bramley's "Desire paths: the illicit trails that defy the urban planners" in *The Guardian* (5 October 2018).

The last line of "Smith Street, 1998" is taken from Juliana Spahr's "poem written after september 11 / 2001" in *This Connection of Everyone with Lungs* (University of California Press, 2005).

The title "What Follows Is a Reconstruction Based on the Best Available Evidence" comes from *Delirious New York* by Rem Koolhaas (The Monacelli Press, 1994). The last line is a transcription of audio from James Coleman's a/v piece "Box (ahhareturnabout), 1977," made up of images and commentary from the 1927 boxing match between Gene Tunney and Jack Dempsey for the world heavyweight title, nicknamed "the long count fight."

The title "Welcome to Fear City: A Survival Guide" comes from a pamphlet called "Welcome to Fear City: A Survival Guide for Visitors to the City of New York" published in June 1975 by The Council for Public Safety, an amalgam of 24 unions of the uniformed services.

"Come Correct" is an English translation of an emoji poem written by Traci Brimhall as part of a poetic collaboration via text message.

"Remember Me as a Time of Day" is the title of a song by the band Explosions in the Sky, and also the name of a painting by Patte Loper.

In "Beyond Which" (my seatbelt is fastened . . .): part eight is partially quoted from the exhibit card for "Die Geliebte (Marz-Gestaltung)" by Curt Ehrhardt at the Museum Boijmans Van Beuningen, and some of part nine is taken from Victor George Mair's "Devastation/Resurrection" at the Bronx Museum of the Arts as cited in the book *In the South Bronx of America* by Mel Rosenthal (Curbstone Press, 2001).

For more extensive resources on the references in this book, and links to the work of the visual artists cited, please see erikameitner.com/books/useful-junk.

Acknowledgments

I am grateful to all the editors of the following journals and anthologies where these poems, sometimes in different form or with different titles, first appeared:

The Adroit Journal: "Missing Parts";
The American Literary Review: "Elegy with Lo-Fi Selfie";
American Poetry Review: "The Last Decade of the 20th Century";
Ampersand Review: "Seven Fragments About Christmas and an Episode of Night Swimming";
The Arkansas International: "Welcome to Fear City: A Survival Guide";
The Believer: "My List of True Facts";
Bennington Review: "This Volatile Taxonomy";
BOAAT: "Are You Popular? (1947)";
Copper Nickel: "A Temple of the Spirit";
Crazyhorse: "Médium Adam 25," "we used to go to the Bulgarian Bar but not together";
Forklift, Ohio: "Selfie with Airplane Voyeurism & References to Your Body," "All the Past and Futures," "Aubade with Projector," "All the Secrets and Holes";
Four Way Review: "Come Correct";
Gulf Coast: "Letter in the Time of Junkmail";
Image: "Letter on Gratitude";
Memorious: "Remember Me as a Time of Day";
New England Review: "The Practice of Depicting Matter as It Passes from Radiance to Decomposition";
Pleiades: "Swift Trucks";
Poem-a-Day, The Academy of American Poets: "Ghost Eden," "What Follows Is a Reconstruction Based on the Best Available Evidence," "A Brief Ontological Investigation";
Poet Lore: "The Seeming Impenetrability of the Space Between," "Nude Selfie Ode," "the bureau of reclamation," "the experience we are thrust into";
Poet's Country: "letter from around the way";
Southern Indiana Review: "The Replication Machine";

The Southern Review: "from this thought a hazy question," "Invitation to Tender";

TAB: The Journal of Poetry & Poetics: "Now That I Can See the Light";

Tampa Review: "Beyond Which" ("The Irish photographer . . .");

Territory: "Beyond Which" ("my seatbelt is fastened . . .");

Tinderbox: "Smith Street, 1998";

Virginia Quarterly Review: "Eternity Now" (as "When the cathedrals were made of plastic");

Washington Square Review: "I would like to be the *you* in someone's poem."

"Letter to Hillary on the Radical Hospitality of the Body" was first published in *The Eloquent Poem*, edited by Gabriel Fried and Elise Paschen (New York: Persea Books, 2019).

"An Occupation of Loss" was first published in *Waterproof: Evidence of a Miami Worth Remembering*, edited by Mario Alejandro Ariza (Miami, FL: Jai Alai Books, 2021).

"the bureau of reclamation" also appeared in *What Things Cost: an anthology for the people*, edited by Rebecca Gayle Howell and Ashley M. Jones (Lexington, KY: The University Press of Kentucky, 2022).

This book would not exist at all in any form, for a variety of reasons, without Keetje Kuipers, Danielle Pafunda, Anna Barry-Jester, and Hillary Adler—muses, editors, cheerleaders, co-conspirators, and partners in creative projects. Special thanks to Sandra Beasley, Jenny Browne, Matthew Guenette, Jason Schneiderman, and Rachel Zucker for all the things, including poem input—and Conor Bracken, Tali Cohen, Camille Dungy, Laura Eve Engel, Joy Katz, Michele Kotler, Brenna Munro, Paisley Rekdal, Sally Rosenthal, Robin Beth Schaer, Evan Simko-Bednarski, Jennie Tranter, and Rachel Lin Weaver for artistic encouragement and moral support. And big thanks to my Virginia Tech academic women's writing group for showing up over and over.

For the time and space to complete this book, I am indebted to Bethany Arts Community, the Hermitage Artist Retreat, the Virginia Center for the

Creative Arts, and the Writer's Room at The Betsy. Thanks to Virginia Tech's English Department, and College of Liberal Arts and Human Sciences for research support that enabled me to write these poems.

I am grateful to Nat Jacks at Inkwell Management, and to Peter Conners and the entire fabulous team at BOA Editions, including Sandy Knight and Richard Foerster, for bringing this book to life; I am so glad to be a part of the BOA family. Much gratitude to Genesis Belanger and Perrotin New York for cover art and images. And lastly, immeasurable thanks to my kids, for putting up with my peripatetic poetic ways, and to Steve Trost for his love and support, and for always unconditionally making space for my work—it would not have been possible to write this book without him.

About the Author

Erika Meitner is the author of six books of poems, including *Ideal Cities* (HarperCollins, 2010), which was a 2009 National Poetry Series winner; *Copia* (BOA Editions, 2014); *Holy Moly Carry Me* (BOA Editions, 2018), which won the 2018 National Jewish Book Award in Poetry, and was a finalist for the National Book Critics Circle Award; and *Useful Junk* (BOA Editions, 2022). Meitner's poems have been anthologized widely, and have appeared in publications including *Virginia Quarterly Review*, *The New York Times Magazine*, *Orion*, *The New Republic*, *Poetry*, *The Southern Review*, and *The Believer*. Other honors include fellowships from MacDowell, the Wisconsin Institute for Creative Writing, the Virginia Center for the Creative Arts, the Hermitage Artist Retreat, Bethany Arts Community, and Blue Mountain Center. She was also the 2015 US-UK Fulbright Distinguished Scholar in Creative Writing at the Seamus Heaney Centre for Poetry at Queen's University Belfast. Meitner is currently a professor of English at Virginia Tech. For more information about Erika Meitner, visit erikameitner.com.

BOA Editions, Ltd. American Poets Continuum Series

Colophon

BOA Editions, Ltd., a not-for-profit publisher of poetry and other literary works, fosters readership and appreciation of contemporary literature. By identifying, cultivating, and publishing both new and established poets and selecting authors of unique literary talent, BOA brings high-quality literature to the public. Support for this effort comes from the sale of its publications, grant funding, and private donations.

○   ○   ○

The publication of this book is made possible, in part,
by the support of the following individuals:

Anonymous
Blue Flower Arts
Bernadette Catalana
Christopher C. Dahl, *in memory of J. D. McClatchy*
Robert & Rae Gilson
James Long Hale
Kelly Hatton
Margaret Heminway
Sandi Henschel
Nora A. Jones
Paul LaFerriere & Dorrie Parini
Jack & Gail Langerak
John & Barbara Lovenheim
Joe McElveney
Boo Poulin
Deborah Ronnen
David W. Ryon
William Waddell & Linda Rubel
Michael Waters & Mihaela Moscaliuc